The big 5
and other wild animals

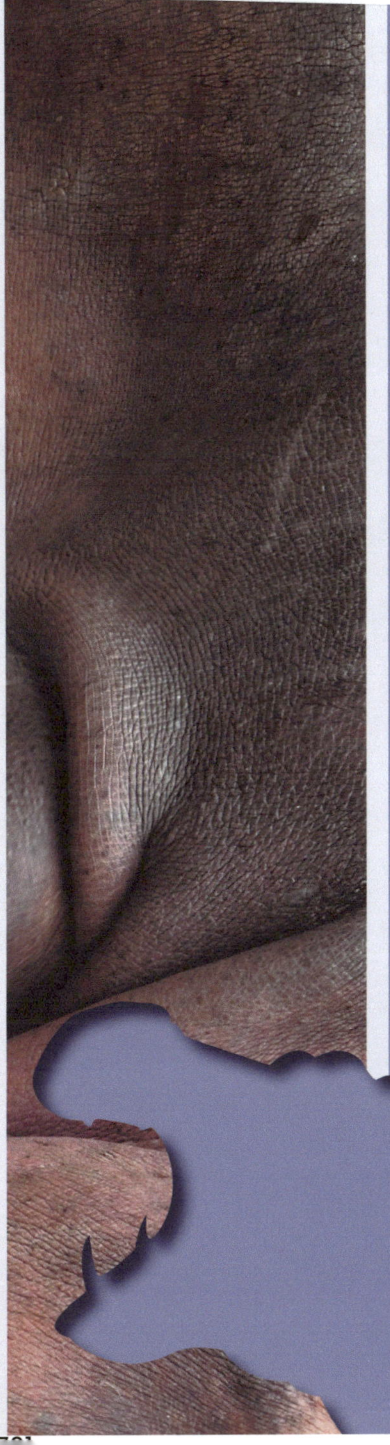

Hippo
Megan Emmett

The big 5 and other wild animals series is published by
Awareness Publishing Group (Pty) Ltd.
Copyright © 2019

Awareness Publishing (SA) (Pty) Ltd
www.awareness.co.za
info@awareness.co.za
+27 (0)86 110 1491
www.facebook.com/AwarenessPublishing

First edition, 2019

Hippo by Megan Emmett
ISBN 978-0-6393-0007-8

Summary: An introduction to the hippo, a wild animal. This book looks at the hippo's physical characteristics, its daily activities, and its family life. The book also talks about the conservation of hippos.

Book design: Dana Espag and Bianca Keenan-Smith.

Editorial credits: Educational consultant: Gillian Mervis. Copy editor: Danya Ristić. Proofreader: Lynda Gilfillan. Picture editor: Anne Laing. Indexer: Lois C Henderson.

Illustrations: Cartoons: Gerhard Cruywagen of Greenhouse Cartoons, and Dana Espag.

Photo credits: Cover and pp.8 (top and bottom), 14, 15 (top and bottom), 20, 28, 29 and 32 © Anne Laing; pp.3 (top and middle), 4, 6, 7 (bottom), 15 (middle),18, 19, 33, 34, and 42 © Shem Compion; p.3 (bottom) © Lucas Photo / Shutterstock; p.7 (top), 10, 24, 25 and 26 © Megan Emmett / Aquavision; p.11 © mountainpix / Shutterstock; p.12 © Tom Brakefield / Great Stock / Corbis; p.16 © Alamy Images / AfriPics; p.21 © O.M / Shutterstock; p.22 © Tom Brakefield / Great Stock / Corbis; p.30 (top) © Tom Brakefield / Great Stock / Corbis; (bottom) © through-my-lens / iStockphoto; p.36 © Richard Du Toit / Gallo Images; p.38 © Sergio Dionisio / Gallo Images; p.39 © Bobby-Jo Clow / Gallo Images; p.40 © http://herculessafaris.com/.

You can read more by Megan Emmett about animals in the book *Game Ranger in Your Backpack – All-in-one Interpretative Guide to the Lowveld*, published by Briza Publications (2010, Pretoria). ISBN 978-1-920217-06-8.

Awareness Publishing
Group

1357908642

Quick facts

Height (at the shoulder)	140 centimetres
Weight	Male: 3 000 kilograms, or three tons Female: 1 500 kilograms, or one and a half tons
Lifespan	About 40 years
Gestation (pregnancy)	Eight months
Number of young	One at a time
Habitat	Water, for example rivers and dams
Food	Grass
Predators	Crocodiles, lions, hyenas and humans. It is mostly the young who are killed – the adults are often too big to be attacked
Is it one of the Big Five?	No! But it is one of the biggest animals in the bush

Hippo is short for hippopotamus. The word hippopotamus comes from the Greek word *hippo*, meaning "horse", and *potamios*, meaning "river". So hippopotamus means "horse of the river".

Words that appear in the text in bold, **like this**, are explained in the Glossary at the end of this book. Some key words are in colour.

Hippos have huge bodies that bulge in the middle. Their heads are big and heavy, and they have four big toes on each foot.

Meet the hippo

After elephants and rhinos, the hippopotamus is the largest land animal in the world. Hippos have big, grey bodies that are shaped like barrels, with a bulge in the middle. They have huge heads, and can open their jaws extremely wide. Hippos have large, flat feet with four pointed toes.

Because hippos live mostly in water, their eyes, noses and ears are high up on the top of their heads. Hippos stay in water so that they can keep cool. With their eyes, noses and ears on top of their heads, hippos can stay in the water while watching and listening for danger.

It is hard to tell the difference between male and female hippos. They look the same, and the males' testicles are hidden inside their bodies, where you cannot see them. So the only way to tell a male from a female is by their size – the males are usually bigger than the females.

A hippo's footprint in the sand, showing its four toes.

When a hippo is in water, sometimes all you can see are its eyes, ears and nostrils.

*When the weather is cold, hippos lie in
the sun to keep their bodies warm.*

*The calf, on the left, has climbed onto
its mother's back to bask in the sun.*

The hippo's skin

Hippos become hot and lose water from their bodies quickly. Also, their skin easily becomes sunburnt. To stay cool and to stop their skin from burning, hippos keep their bodies underwater most of the time. Sometimes, only the hippos' nostrils are above the water.

When the weather is cold, hippos lie in the sun to get warm. We call this basking. Hippos **bask** often in winter. Calves, or baby hippos, get cold more quickly than adult hippos do. Sometimes, while it is in the water, a calf climbs onto its mother's back to bask in the sun. This helps the calf to warm up.

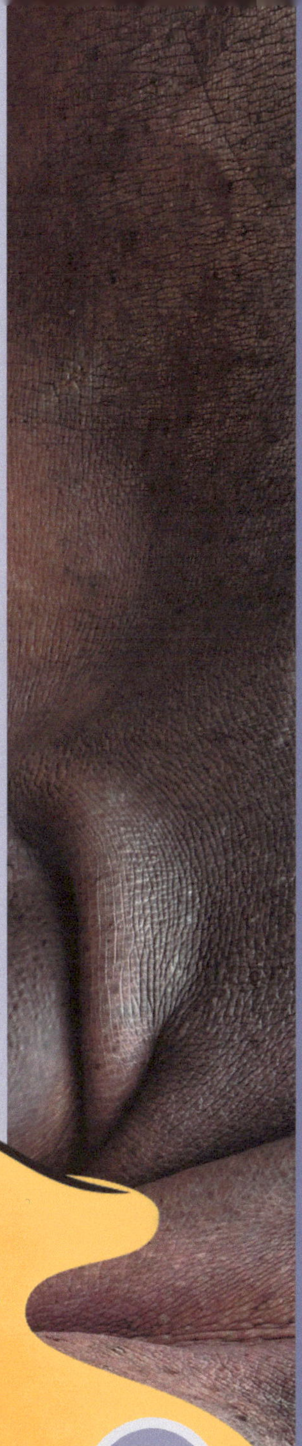

When there is not much rain, hippos pack tightly into pools of water to stay wet.

Getting too hot

When there is a **drought** and there is no rain for a long time, dams and rivers have little or no water. This means that a hippo cannot cover itself in water, and the hippo's skin may become badly sunburnt. The hippo makes, or **secretes**, red liquid that looks like blood. The red liquid acts as a sunscreen. This liquid protects the hippo for a short time, but then the hippo's skin soon dries out again and cracks.

Sometimes during a drought hippos pack together in muddy pools. They do this so that their skin will stay wet. But when they lie close to each other, they become bad-tempered and they fight. At night, when there is no sun, hippos travel long distances to look for deeper water.

Mother hippos sometimes stand over their calves to make shade for them. This helps to keep the calves cool. If the weather is very hot, the mother hippo will **dribble** spit, or saliva, onto her calf to keep its skin wet and cool.

Drops of red liquid on a hippo's skin that act as a sunscreen lotion, when there is little or no water for the hippo to stand in.

11

This hippo may look like it is swimming, but it is actually walking underwater, along a riverbed.

Living in water

Hippos do not swim in the water. They walk on the bottom, or bed, of a river or dam. Before they go underwater, hippos exhale, breathing out most of the air from their lungs. Having less air in their lungs helps them to stay under the water while they walk. If they have too much air in their lungs, they float up to the top of the water again. When hippos want to come up to the surface, they push themselves off the riverbed with their feet. This movement sometimes makes them look as if they are swimming.

Hippos cannot breathe when they are underwater. They have to come up to the surface to breathe. Hippos can stay under the water for five or six minutes at a time. Even very young baby hippos can stay under for as long as 40 seconds.

When hippos go underwater, they pinch their nostrils closed and they fold their ears down. This stops the water from getting inside their noses and their ears.

13

By lying in the water all day, hippos save energy for grazing at night.

Water saves energy

All living creatures need **energy** to live. We use energy for many things – for example, when we move, breathe and think. People and animals get energy from the food that they eat. Most big animals have to eat a lot of food, because they need a lot of energy.

Hippos are very big animals, but they do not eat a lot of food. Animals that live and walk on land need more energy than animals that live in water. Hippos are land animals but because they spend so much time in water, they save energy and do not need to eat as much as other land animals.

A hippo eats about 15 to 40 kilograms of grass in one night. Other land animals that are the same size as a hippo, for example a young female elephant, eat about 125 kilograms of food every day.

Hippos come out of the water to feed on grass at night to avoid getting sunburnt.

Feeding at night

Hippos feed on land at night. They eat when it is dark so that they do not get sunburnt. Hippos usually come out of the water in the late afternoon or early evening, when the temperature has cooled down. Sometimes they come out only when it is completely dark.

Hippos walk along the same paths every night. They do not look for a new path to get to their food. Hippos also do not travel far from the water. They usually walk only one or two kilometres away, and they return to the water early in the morning, before the sun is hot.

If hippos have to walk far, they will do so. Hippos will travel 15 kilometres in a night if they need to find food – for example, in a time of drought.

Sometimes hippo eat plants that grow in water.

The hippo's food

Hippos are grazers – they eat grass. They use their wide lips to pluck and pull the grass. They are not fussy and do not mind which part of the grass they eat. After hippos have grazed, the grass that is left behind is short. Hippos often return to the same place to feed, night after night. They are noisy when they eat, making loud chewing sounds.

Hippos live together in the water, but they feed alone. Only a female hippo, or cow, and her calf will feed together.

Sometimes, hippos get hungry while they are in the water during the day. When they do, they eat the plants that grow and float in rivers and dams.

Hippos come out of the water to eat grass. They do not mind the birds that walk nearby. The birds look for and eat any insects that the hippo may have disturbed while it is grazing.

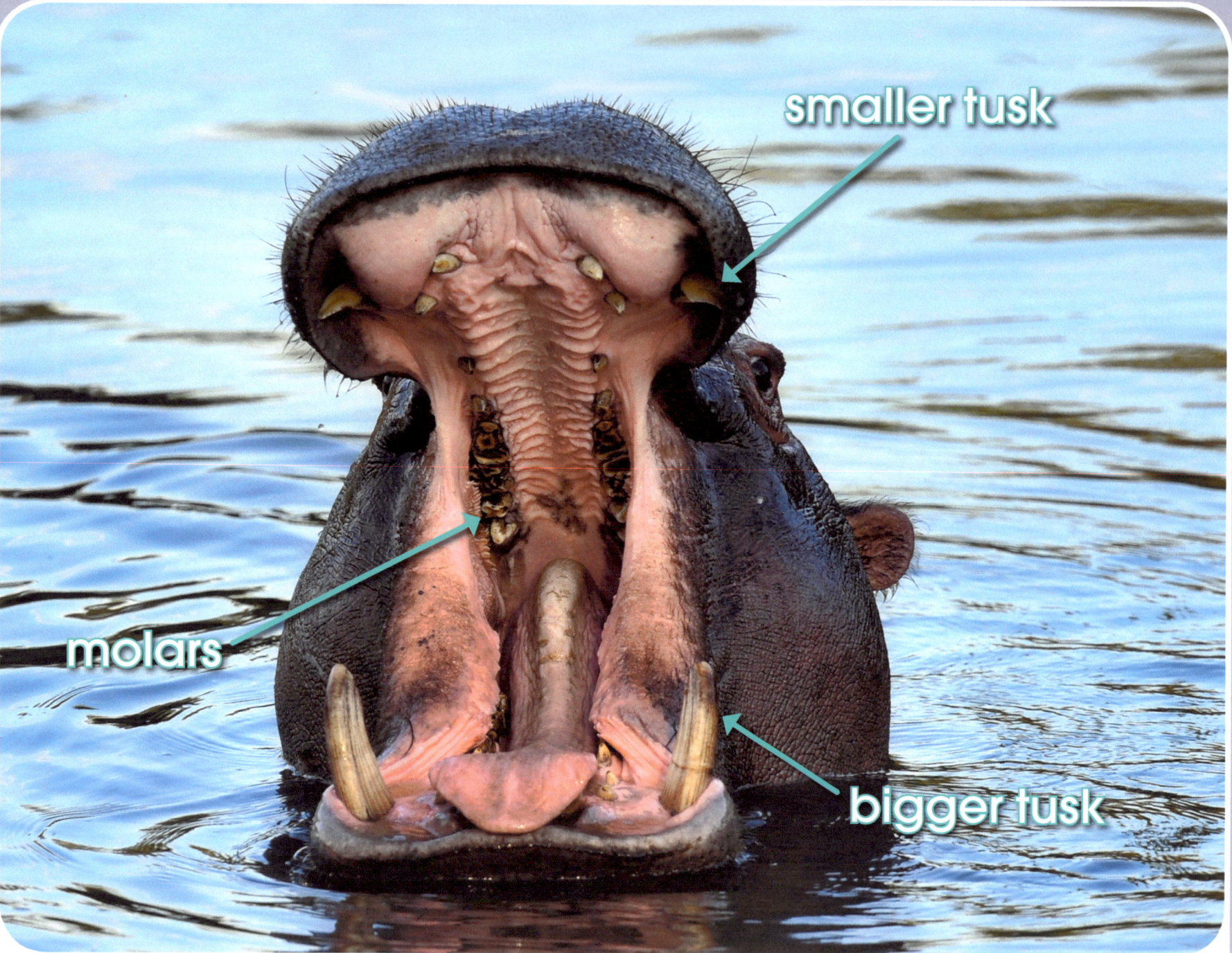

smaller tusk

molars

bigger tusk

A hippo has smaller tusks on its upper jaw, molars at the back, and bigger, longer tusks on its bottom jaw.

The hippo's teeth

Hippos chew their food with big, flat teeth called molars. These teeth are at the back of their mouths. We also have molars at the back of our mouths, which we use for chewing.

Hippos have long, sharp teeth in the front of their mouths. These teeth at the front of a hippo's bottom jaw are bigger than the front teeth on the top. We call these large teeth tusks. The tusks of a male hippo, or bull, are bigger than a female's tusks.

The sharpened edge of a bottom tusk.

A hippo's tusks keep growing until the hippo dies. An old hippo may have tusks that are 30 to 50 centimetres long. Tusks of 50 centimetres, or half a metre, are extremely long!

A hippo uses its tusks to protect itself and its young. With its tusks, the hippo attacks **predators** such as lions and crocodiles. A hippo has such strong jaws that it can bite a three-metre crocodile in half! When bull hippos fight with each other, they often hurt and injure each other with their tusks.

As a hippo opens and closes its mouth, the tusks on the top rub against the tusks at the bottom. This rubbing makes all four tusks very sharp. The sharpened tusks can then easily cut into the skin of another hippo, even though a hippo's skin may be six centimetres thick.

21

A hippo running quickly towards a river. Its skin is cut and scarred from fighting.
A scared hippo may charge and run over anything in its path.

Escaping danger

Hippos feed at night, on land. If they become frightened while they are eating, they run straight back into the water. Hippos feel safe in the water because lions cannot catch them there.

When hippos run back to the water, they run along the path that they know and are familiar with. This is the same path that takes them to the area where they feed. These paths are wide, with no bushes or rocks that get in the hippos' way. Hippos cannot jump, so they need a clear path that they can use to run back to the water. They run along these paths very quickly. Hippos are big, heavy animals, but they can run at speeds of up to 36 kilometres per hour when they need to!

When hippos are frightened, they often **charge** at and attack their enemy. Hippos sometimes charge humans, too. A hippo gets very scared if it sees a person walking along its path. The hippo runs from where it is feeding, and may trample the person by running them over and squashing them. Many people have died in this way.

Stamping out fires

There is an old story, or myth, that hippos stamp out campfires with their feet. This is because hippos run back to the water when they are afraid, and if someone lit a campfire on their path, they may run over the fire, stamping it out with their feet as they run. People like camping near water, but this is a bad idea if there are hippos nearby!

a red-billed oxpecker

Hippos and birds

Birds called oxpeckers often sit on a hippo's back or head. There are two types of these birds. Red-billed oxpeckers have completely red beaks. Yellow-billed oxpeckers have some red and some yellow on their beaks. Oxpeckers eat ticks that are on the hippo's skin. Ticks are parasites that bite through the hippo's skin and suck its blood. By dealing with the ticks, oxpeckers and hippos help each other: the hippos are clean and are free of ticks, and the oxpeckers have a meal.

Hippos live together in pods. The females and calves rest close to one another.

Living together

A group of hippos is called a pod of hippos, or a herd of hippos. There can be two hippos or 2 000 hippos in a pod! If there is a lot of water in an area, there will be many hippos. But if there is not much water in an area, only a few hippos will live there. Usually, there are eight to 12 hippos in a pod.

In every pod, there is usually only one male or bull hippo. Bulls protect their own parts of the river. A bull will not let other bulls come near the part that belongs to him. We call this his territory. A bull allows cows and their calves to live in his territory. There may be more than one pod of female and baby hippos in a bull's territory.

In rivers where there are hippo, a bull guards the part of the river that is his territory.

Bulls are grumpy animals. They easily become angry and fight with other bulls, chasing them from their territory. Even young bulls that do not have territories can be injured by older bulls. The older bulls' sharp teeth cut the young bulls' heads and shoulders.

Hippos in a pod make different sounds. They honk, growl, grunt and squeal. Each sound has a message. For example, a hippo may grunt at another hippo to tell it to move out of the way.

Two bull hippo face each other to fight. One wiggles his tail to spread his dung in the water, and opens his jaw to show his big teeth. The other responds by also showing off his teeth.

Keeping other hippos away

A bull hippo makes sure that other hippos know where his territory is. The bull scatters his dung, or waste matter, against bushes that grow along the banks of the river or dam. As the bull **defecates**, or gives off his dung, he wiggles his tail from side to side. This wiggling spreads his dung in every direction. When other bulls see and smell this dung, they know that they must stay away from the territory.

Bulls also scatter their dung when they meet each other. First they stop and look at each other, and then they defecate. As the bulls defecate, they wiggle their tails and their dung flies around. At the same time, they make a loud noise, like a growl. Usually, one of the bulls becomes frightened and runs away. But if neither of the two bulls runs away, they fight.

27

A hippo bull opening his mouth to show other bulls how big and sharp his tusks are.

Showing who is boss

A bull that is in charge of a herd is called the **dominant** bull. When a bull wants to show other bulls that he is dominant, he opens his mouth in a big yawn. The bull does this so that other hippos can see his huge, sharp tusks. Bulls usually yawn when they are in the water, but at times they also yawn on land. This yawning tells their enemies to stay away.

Sometimes hippo bulls make a honking noise. This honking tells other bulls to keep away from their territory. The honking noise of a hippo is so loud that it can be heard from far away.

This hippo is yawning to frighten other bulls away from his territory.

29

A cow hippo and her calf underwater.

Cow hippos take excellent care of their calves.

Baby hippos

Baby hippos, or calves, are born in **shallow** water. The water must be shallow so that the calf does not drown. Calves can walk and swim just a few minutes after they are born.

Hippo calves drink milk from their mothers. We call this suckling, and older calves can do this under the water. When a calf suckles underwater, it folds its ears down and pinches its nostrils closed. In this way, the calf stops water from going into its ears and nose, and it does not drown.

Mother hippos are extremely protective of their babies. A cow fights with any hippo that comes near her calf. The cow will even fight with a bull. Cows also protect their calves from predators such as lions and crocodiles.

As hippo walk along a riverbed, they make big pathways through the water plants, which helps the river to flow more easily.

Helping the rivers and the bush

Hippos need rivers, but rivers also need hippos. When hippos defecate in rivers or near to them, fish and insects eat the dung. Hippo dung also feeds and **fertilises** the grass, trees and bushes that live along riverbanks, helping these plants to grow.

As hippos walk in the water, they make pathways through plants that grow, sometimes quite densely, in the riverbed. These underwater paths help the river to flow freely.

Hippos are also important animals on land. Together with elephants and rhinos, hippos trample the bush, crushing it under their heavy feet. In this way, these large animals open up the bush, and smaller animals can then make their way through it more easily. Hippos usually eat the longer grass, and then other animals such as wildebeest and zebra eat the shorter grass that the hippos leave behind.

These young wildebeest have just crossed a river.
The hippo helps them to get up onto the riverbank.

Helping other animals

Sometimes hippos help young antelope or buck, such as wildebeest and impala, to cross rivers. The hippos help these animals so that crocodiles and other predators cannot attack them. This is unusual, because different species, or types, of animals do not usually help one another.

We are not sure why hippos try to protect other animals such as antelope. It may be because hippos know that crocodiles are dangerous. They would know this by instinct and from having learnt it by experience. Instinct is something that animals and people know from birth, and that they do not have to learn. But in some areas, adult hippos would have learnt about the danger of crocodiles because crocodiles have eaten their calves. Perhaps hippos know that if they do not help antelope to cross rivers, the antelope could be eaten by crocodiles.

Sometimes, hippos lick the bodies of dead hippos.
They also try to chase away crocodiles that come to eat the dead hippo.

Doing a strange thing

Sometimes hippos do a strange thing: they lick the skin of hippos that have died. We are not sure why they do this.

Salt is an important part of a hippo's diet. Some scientists think that the hippo is trying to lick salt off the dead hippo's skin. Other scientists think that the hippo is trying to eat the dead hippo. But this is difficult to believe, because hippos are herbivores – they usually eat only grass.

Another possible reason for the licking is that the hippos may be trying to recognise and see if they know the dead hippo.

Did you know?

Animals that eat plants as well as meat are called omnivores.

37

Zookeepers with a pygmy hippo calf that is one month old.

The hippo's relatives

The only other animal that is part of the hippo family is the pygmy hippopotamus. The word pygmy comes from the Greek word *pugmaios*, which means "dwarf", or "unusually small". Pygmy hippos are much smaller than other hippos, and they only weigh about 200 kilograms.

Pygmy hippos live in West Africa, either alone or in pairs. They live in swamps, or areas where there is a lot of water, and along streams in forests. Pygmy hippos are difficult to see or find. This is because there are many plants in swamps and forests, and pygmy hippos can hide in this dense **vegetation**. Also, very few pygmy hippos are still alive nowadays.

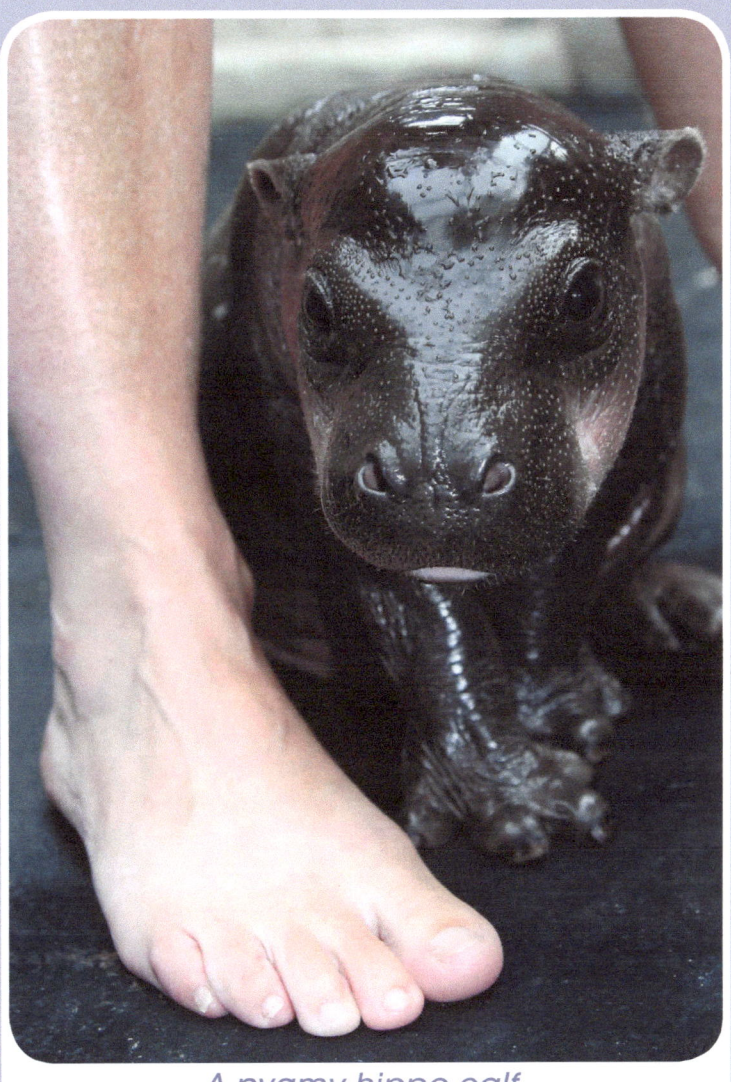

A pygmy hippo calf.

39

These men have shot this hippo for sport.

Hippos in danger

Nowadays, there are still many hippos in South Africa, and in many other African countries. But every year, there are fewer hippos than there were before. We say that hippos are **vulnerable**, which means that they may become extinct in time. When an animal is extinct, there are no more of these animals living in the world.

There are fewer hippos every year for two reasons. First, the places where hippos live keep getting smaller as people build bigger cities and pollute, or poison, more rivers with garbage and chemicals. In South Africa, hippos live mostly in game reserves.

Second, people kill hippos for various reasons. They may be afraid of a hippo. They may want to eat the hippo, or sell the hippo meat. Sometimes, they hunt hippos just as a sport. People also kill hippos so that they can use the animals' teeth for making knife handles and other carvings to sell to tourists.

A hippo splashing in a river.

Glossary

bask – to lie in the sun to get warm

charge – to attack by running straight towards a person or another animal

defecates – releases or gives off solid waste matter from the body

dominant – stronger and more important

dribble – to let saliva or spit run out of the mouth

drought – a long period of time with little or no rain, which results in a shortage of water

energy – the power or strength that people and animals get from the food that they eat

fertilises – provides food for a plant to grow

predators – animals that hunt and kill other animals for food

secretes – releases through the skin as a liquid

shallow – not deep, for example a part of a dam or river where there is not much water

territory – the specific area where an animal, or group of animals, lives

vegetation – the plants that grow in a specific area

vulnerable – animals that are in danger of becoming extinct, or dying out

www.ingramcontent.com/pod-product-compliance
Lightning Source LLC
Chambersburg PA
CBHW041323290426

44108CB00004B/111